That's hot, folks!

THE COLMAN'S MUSTARD COOKBOOK

PAUL HARTLEY

ABSOLUTE PRESS

In association with
www.breakfastandbrunch.com
www.deliontheweb.co.uk

First published in Great Britain
in 2004
by **Absolute Press**
Scarborough House
29 James Street West
Bath BA1 2BT
Phone 44 (0) 1225 316013
Fax 44 (0) 1225 445836
E-mail info@absolutepress.co.uk
Website www.absolutepress.co.uk

Publisher Jon Croft
Commissioning Editor Meg Avent
Designer Matt Inwood

A catalogue record of this book
is available from the British Library

Reprinted 2007.

ISBN 13: 9781904573159

Printed and bound by
1010 International, China

CONTENTS

IN 1901, CAPTAIN ROBERT FALCON SCOTT SET SAIL ON DISCOVERY, HEADED FOR ANTARCTICA. HE TOOK WITH HIM PROVISIONS OF SALT BEEF, FISH STEAKS AND

PENGUIN FILLETS. HE NEEDED A CONDIMENT THAT WOULD LIVEN UP HIS MEALS... HE TOOK A TON AND A HALF OF COLMAN'S ENGLISH MUSTARD.

It's nicer with
MUSTARD

THE COLMAN'S MUSTARD RECIPE COLLECTION

Butterfly Lamb with Honey and Mustard

3kg leg of lamb, gross weight
(ask your butcher to prepare
a butterflied leg of lamb)

For the marinade
150ml soy sauce
8 cm fresh ginger, grated
2 tablespoons runny honey
4 cloves of garlic, finely chopped
1 level tablespoon Colman's
English mustard powder
Freshly ground black pepper
25ml olive oil

1 Place the lamb in a suitable big dish or roasting tray. Mix together all the other ingredients. Spoon the mixture evenly over the lamb and leave overnight in the fridge. It is even better if left for up to two days.

2 Remove the lamb from the fridge one hour before cooking. Set the oven on high (200C/400F/Gas 6). Take the lamb out of the marinade and dry it with some kitchen paper. Open it out fully and flatten with the palm of your hand. Now place the lamb in a roasting dish and put it into the very hot oven for 20-30 minutes until the fat just begins to crisp. Remove from the oven, cover with foil and leave to rest for 10 minutes.

3 Now for the good bit. Heat the remaining marinade slowly, do not allow it to boil. Thickly slice the lamb and ladle the marinade over. Perfect served with crispy potato wedges cooked in goose fat, a dish of fresh green beans or mixed green salad. This makes a great dinner party, Sunday lunch or barbecue dish.

SERVES 6-8

In the beginning...

■■■ The origins of mustard date back to the sixth century BC: Pythagoras is said to have used it as an antidote to scorpion stings. A hundred years later, the pioneering Greek physician Hippocrates used the seed for making a variety of medicines and poultices.

■■■ The potent nature of the mustard seed was attested to in an exchange between King Darius of Persia and the young Alexander the Great. Darius gifted Alexander a sack of sesame seed to represent the number of his army. Alexander returned the compliment, with a sack of mustard seeds to symbolise both the number and the fiery nature of his army.

Tequila Prawns with Mustard and Lime

500g large cooked prawns
1 yellow pepper cut into 1.5cm
    pieces
8 salad onions
    (white bulb part only)
16 cherry tomatoes

For the marinade
30ml Tequila
Juice 1 lime
1 teaspoon Colman's English
    mustard

1 whole lime, cut into 8 wedges

**You will need 8 wooden kebab
    skewers.**

1 Soak the kebab skewers in water to prevent the ends burning during cooking. Spear the prawns, peppers, onions and tomatoes alternately onto the skewers. Place the kebabs in a shallow dish.

2 To make the marinade, blend the Tequila, lime juice and mustard and pour it over the prawn kebabs. Cover and chill for 30 minutes, turning the kebabs from time to time to take up the juices.

3 Fire up the barbie and cook the kebabs for 3-4 minutes on each side, basting with the juices of the marinade. Serve each kebab with a wedge of lime, leaving the cook to enjoy the rest of the Tequila accompanied, in time honoured tradition, with a little lime and salt.

SERVES 4

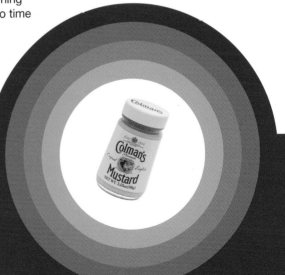

■■■ The word 'mustard' is thought to derive from the Latin words 'must' (much) and 'ardens' (burning).

Crispy Pork with Pink Champagne and Passionfruit

6 trimmed pieces pork belly, about 200 to 250g, preferably square and scored by your butcher

12 banana shallots, peeled and halved

6 cloves garlic, peeled and sliced

2 dessertspoons Colman's English mustard powder

25g flour

1 stock cube, dissolved in 1 litre water

37.5cl pink Champagne (or sparkling rosé)

1 tablespoon sea salt

3 passionfruit, halved and flesh removed

1 Heat a deep frying pan on the hob and place the belly pork fat-side down for about 5 minutes to tease out the fat. Turn the pork belly pieces once there is enough juice for them to sit in. Add the halved banana shallots and the garlic to the frying pan and continue to cook on a medium heat for a further 8-10 minutes until the shallots begin to caramelise.

2 Meanwhile, mix the mustard, flour and half the stock in a separate jug, whisking until no lumps remain. Pour the mixture over the pork belly with the remaining stock and the Champagne. Transfer everything to a roasting tin, cover with foil and place in a pre-heated oven at 180C/350F/Gas 5 for 1½ hours.

3 Remove the roasting tray from the oven and take out the belly pork and place on a new oven tray. Pour all the remaining juices into a sauce pan and set aside. Sprinkle the pork belly with sea salt and return to a hot oven 230C/450F/Gas 8 for 15-20 minutes to crisp up the pork.

4 Meanwhile, heat the pan of Champagne juices adding the passion fruit flesh, mix together well and continue to simmer until the sauce has reduced enough to be able to coat the back of a spoon. Place the pork on a warmed serving plate and serve the Champagne sauce around the pork.

SERVES 6

Fennel Coleslaw with Colman's Mustard Mayonnaise

750g fresh fennel, greenery removed and finely sliced
1 large onion, finely sliced
2 large carrots, peeled and grated
1 tablespoon small capers
1 tablespoon diced dill pickle
4 tablespoons mayonnaise (preferably home-made)
1 tablespoon Colman's English mustard
1 teaspoon lemon juice
Olive oil
Salt and freshly ground black pepper
1 dessertspoon vermouth
1 teaspoon sesame seeds, toasted
50g fresh coriander, chopped

1 Place the sliced fennel, onion and grated carrots into a big mixing bowl, add the capers and diced dill pickle.

2 In a separate dish mix together the mayonnaise, mustard, lemon juice, 2 teaspoons of olive oil, a pinch or two of salt and some freshly ground black pepper. Finally add the vermouth and mix all together with a wooden spoon until you have a smooth, creamy dressing.

3 Spoon the dressing over the salad and mix together thoroughly. Place the dressed salad into a clean dish and sprinkle with the sesame seeds and the coriander.

4 This makes a great accompaniment to fish, barbecued pork or bangers and mash.

SERVES 4

HOT FACT

The town of Al Aziziyah in Libya, 20 miles inland of the country's capital, Tripoli, is the place where the hottest world temperature in history was recorded. On September 13th, 1922, thermometers in the town peaked at a blistering 136° Fahrenheit (57.8° Celsius). A road runs from the town into the Sahara Desert, where a burning wind called the 'ghibli' – one intensely hot and strewn with sand – can soar temperatures up to between 40 and 50°C within the space of sixty minutes.

Orange-spiced Chocolate Cookies

100g dark cooking chocolate
50g salted butter, softened
100g soft brown sugar
$1/2$ teaspoon ground cinnamon
1 teaspoon Colman's English
   mustard powder
150g plain flour
2 teaspoons baking powder
1 medium free-range egg, beaten
1 tablespoon Grand Marnier
   liqueur
Zest 1 medium orange

1 Melt the chocolate in a bowl over a pan of boiling water and then set aside. Into a food mixer, put the softened butter, sugar, cinnamon and mustard powder. Sieve in the flour and baking powder and add the egg. Mix together and, after about 30 seconds, slowly add the melted chocolate. Finally, add the Grand Marnier liqueur and the orange zest and again mix together at the slowest speed until you have a dough like consistency.

2 Place a large piece of greaseproof paper onto the worktop and gently roll out the dough to about 3cm thick. Using a biscuit cutter begin to cut out the biscuits, re-rolling until all the dough has been used. Leaving the biscuits on the greaseproof paper, transfer them to the fridge to chill for about 2 hours. Once chilled, place in a pre-heated oven at 190C/ 375F/Gas 5 for 8 minutes. Leave to cool before serving. Surprisingly good on cold winter days or with tea in the garden. The mustard gives the whole recipe a real lift.

MAKES 20 COOKIES

Kidneys Devilled with Colman's Mustard

500g lambs' kidneys
12g butter
1 dessertspoon vegetable oil
1 medium onion, finely diced
Worcestershire sauce
100g button mushrooms
55ml Madeira wine
2 heaped teaspoons Colman's
   English mustard powder
Salt and freshly ground black pepper
120ml double cream

1 Cut the kidneys in half and with scissors carefully remove the white centre. Put the butter and oil into a large frying pan and heat until hot (butter for flavour, oil to withstand higher heat).

2 Sauté the onions until transparent, add the kidneys and a dash of Worcestershire sauce and sauté for another 3-4 minutes. Now add the mushrooms and the Madeira and let it all bubble and reduce by about one third.

3 Meanwhile, in a separate bowl mix the cream with the mustard and season with salt and pepper. Remove the kidneys from the heat and allow to cool for about 1 minute. Add the mustard cream and allow to bubble and thicken. Serve on thick granary toast with a sprinkle of chopped parsley, accompanied by a glass of chilled Somerset cider.

SERVES 2

COLD TRUTH

When the woodland frog stumbles upon cold times, he's not one to worry. He calls home a place just north of the Arctic Circle, and when the cold winds come blowing, can survive for weeks in a frozen state. The glucose in his blood acts like a kind of antifreeze that centres on his vital organs, protecting them from damage, but which allows the rest of his body to freeze solid. So, whilst up to 65% of his body water can become frozen, his cells don't – only the water outside the cells. As soon as the outside temperature rises, his body begins to thaw and he's on the move once more.

Cream of Cauliflower & Mustard Soup

50g unsalted butter
1 kg cauliflower (I try to use
    Romanesque for this, as it
    has a lovely nutty flavour)
300g good firm shallots
    (try and locate the purple tinted
    banana shallots)
100g celery
1 heaped dessertspoon garlic,
    finely diced
25g Colman's English mustard
    powder, freshly made
100ml single cream
20g brown sugar
Salt and freshly ground black pepper
1 dessertspoon chopped French
    parsley

1 Melt the butter gently in a pan. When melted, add all the other ingredients apart from 4 small cauliflower florets and the parsley. When the shallots have become transparent and the other vegetables have begun to soften, add 1 litre of cold water and bring the mixture to the boil. Simmer gently for 30 minutes. Allow to cool a little and then blitz in a liquidiser, adding the cream until smooth. Season to taste.

2 Next take the reserved florets and blanch for about 5 minutes. Serve the soup in deep round bowls placing 2 florets in the centre of each bowl. Garnish with the parsley. This is excellent served piping hot in the cold winter months, or chilled during the summer.

SERVES 2

Right Every minute, 45 jars of Colman's Mustard are bought all over the world.

COLMAN'S

MUSTARD

ALL OVER THE WORLD.

Ham & Mustard Pasties

200g potatoes, diced into
  1 cm cubes
150g swede, diced
150g carrot, diced
1 medium onion, diced
450g puff pastry
200g off-cut ham (trimmings
  – see your friendly butcher)
Good dollop Colman's English
  mustard
Good sized sprig parsley,
  finely chopped
Pepper, according to taste
1 egg, beaten

1 In a large saucepan of boiling water, place the potatoes, swede, carrot and onion and boil until al dente. Drain and leave in a colander to cool slightly.

2 Meanwhile, divide the puff pastry into 4 or 8 even squares (depending on the number of pasties required) and roll out to approximately 3-4 mm deep.

3 Trim off any excess fat from the ham, and cut into rustic shaped pieces. Combine the ham with the potato mixture and add the mustard, parsley and pepper.

4 Pre-heat the oven to 190C/375F/Gas 5. Divide the mixture equally between the puff pastry squares. Wet the edges of the pastry and fold the diagonal corners together. Crimp the edge of the pastry to resemble a pasty shape, brush with the beaten egg and refrigerate for 15 minutes. Place on a baking tray and bake in the centre of the oven for approximately 15-20 minutes, (or until an even golden brown). Serve immediately. Perfect with a glass of chilled Somerset farmhouse cider.

MAKES 4 LARGE OR 8 SMALL PASTIES

TV, music... the Vatican...

■■■ In 1996, the J Walter Thompson creative agency developed the now-famous 'Farmyard campaign' featuring animatronic farmyard animals, among whom the indubitable star was the pig. The campaign reached its climax with the 1998 installment which saw our funky pig strutting his stuff and singing lines to the ironic tune of 'Staying Alive'. Pig sang:

'Well you can tell by the way I'm made of pork / I'm not a Colman's fan. I think we should talk.'

The advert was a huge success.

Roasted Parsnips with Mustard and Herbs

4 large parsnips, peeled, quartered lengthways and cores removed

2 level tablespoons plain flour

1 level tablespoon Colman's English mustard powder

1 level teaspoon Parmesan, finely grated

Salt and freshly ground black pepper

1 dessertspoon mixed fresh sage, rosemary and thyme, stalks removed and finely chopped

2 tablespoons vegetable oil or goose fat

1 Pre-heat the oven to 180C/ 350F/Gas 4. In an oblong dish, mix together the flour, mustard, Parmesan, salt and pepper and herbs. Set aside.

2 In a large saucepan par-boil the parsnips for 4-5 minutes, drain, and roll them in the herby, mustard mixture until completely coated. (The coating will stick to the parsnips much better if they are still warm.) Pour about 2 tablespoons of vegetable oil or goose fat into a roasting dish and place in the hot oven for 5 minutes.

3 Remove the pan from the oven and carefully add the seasoned parsnips and baste with the hot fat. Roast for 10-20 minutes until golden brown and scrummy. Wonderful with sliced beef, wild boar or venison as a main course. Also good as a starter, sprinkled with a little lemon zest and served on thin toasted rye bread, spread with a slither of Colman's English mustard. This is a dish best served after the first frost of the year, when parsnips are at their best.

SERVES 4

■■■ 'Mustard's no good without roast beef.'
Chico Marx, *Funny Business*.
■■■ 'Mean Mister Mustard sleeps in the park /
Shaves in the dark trying to save paper'
From the Beatles' 'Mean Mr Mustard'.
■■■ Pope John XXII was said to be fond of mustard.

Cheese Soufflé

50g fresh breadcrumbs
40g butter (you will need extra
   butter to grease the cooking
   dishes)
25g flour
300ml hot milk
4 eggs, separated
400g good tasty crumbled cheese
   like Shropshire Blue or
   Montgomery Cheddar
Cracked black pepper
6 grates fresh nutmeg
3 to 4 dashes Tabasco sauce
Pinch cayenne
4 spring onions, finely chopped
2 tablespoons Colman's English
   mustard
Parmesan, grated, for sprinkling

**You will need 6 individual
ramekins or one 25cm
souffle dish.**

1 Pre-heat the oven 200C/ 400F/Gas 6. Butter the soufflé dish and sprinkle the bottom and sides with some of the fresh breadcrumbs (these help the soufflé to 'climb up').

2 To make the roux, melt the butter in a small pan over a low heat. Remove the pan from the heat and add the flour and beat until smooth and lump free. Return to the heat for about 3 minutes. Remove the pan from the heat and stir in half the milk and beat until smooth. Add the remaining milk and simmer for 10 minutes until thick and smooth. Take off the stove and allow to cool.

3 Beat the egg yolks lightly and add them to the pan. Stir in the crumbled cheese, pepper, nutmeg, Tabasco, cayenne, spring onions and mustard.

4 Whisk the 4 egg whites with a pinch of salt to form soft peaks and then fold the egg whites into the sauce. Pour this into the ramekins or the soufflé dish and sprinkle with the remaining breadcrumbs and the Parmesan. Bake the soufflé for 30-40 minutes until it looks like a chef's hat. Serve immediately, either on it's own as a starter or with a bowl of garden-fresh green vegetables as a main course. Please note that a good soufflé should be runny and soft in the centre and firm on the outside.

SERVES 6

Right Howzat! One of five Victorian souvenir Colman's Mustard cricket cards.

Three Fish Pie with Peas, Cheese and Mustard

Make up 600g of fish with
200g natural smoked haddock
200g white cod
200g raw prawns

5 large potatoes, peeled and
    quartered
30g butter
240ml double cream
2 medium free-range eggs
1 large onion, finely chopped
Olive oil for frying
100g frozen petit pois
2 large handfuls fresh spinach,
    chopped
3 tablespoons strong mature
    Cheddar, grated
2 heaped teaspoons Colman's
    English mustard
1 heaped tablespoon of flat-leaf
    parsley, finely chopped
Salt and freshly ground black
    pepper

Ask your fishmonger to fillet and pin-bone the haddock and cod.

1 Slice the fish into 2.5cm strips, leaving the prawns whole.

2 In a large saucepan of boiling salted water, cook the potatoes until soft. Drain and mash with the butter, half the cream and season to taste. While the spuds are cooking, boil the eggs for 8 minutes, then cool them and peel and quarter.

3 Fry the onion in a little olive oil until just transparent. Remove from the heat and add the remainder of the double cream, peas, spinach, cheese, mustard and parsley, allow to cool to room temperature. When cool, pour into an ovenproof dish. Finally, drop in the fish and season, then layer the eggs and top with the mashed potato.

4 Place in a pre-heated oven at 180C/350F/Gas 4 for 25-30 minutes until the potato is golden brown. Serve with a shower of parsley.

SERVES 6

Venison Sausage Potato Puff

8 venison sausages
4 large potatoes
25g butter
3 eggs, separated
Salt and freshly ground black pepper
1 level tablespoon freshly chopped
    parsley
4 tablespoons of Colman's English
    mustard
50ml double cream

1 Turn the grill to medium and lightly grill the venison sausages until cooked. Meanwhile, peel the potatoes, cut them into quarters and boil in lightly salted water until cooked. Drain and return them to the pan, adding the butter, egg yolks, salt and pepper, the parsley and the mustard. Whisk thoroughly with an electric beater, slowly adding the cream. Set aside.

2 In a separate bowl, whisk the egg whites into soft peaks and carefully fold in the mashed potato. Grease an ovenproof dish, spread half of the potato mixture onto the bottom of the dish, cover with the grilled sausages and top with the rest of the potato. Bake in a moderate oven (180C/350F/ Gas 4) for about 20 to 25 minutes until the potato has become brown. Serve hot with Countryman's Piccalilli (see page 28) and a tomato and basil salad.

SERVES 4

HOT FACT

The long, hot UK summer of 1976 culminated in the biggest drought and highest temperatures since records began in 1727. A hose pipe ban was enforced in late spring and the Government even went so far as to appoint a Minister of Drought, in a desperate effort to alleviate the problem. Temporary taps – standpipes – had to be erected in badly affected areas to continue the supply of water. From the 23rd of June, in various parts of the UK, temperatures exceeded 32°C (90°F) for 15 consecutive days.

Mustard Mousseline

50g butter
4 medium free-range egg yolks
2 tablespoons lemon juice
2 tablespoons cold water
1 tablespoon Colman's English
mustard

1 Place the butter, egg yolks, lemon juice and water in a bowl. Place the bowl in a bain marie. (If you don't have a bain marie you can make one by putting a bowl over a saucepan of simmering water, making sure the bowl does not touch the water.) Now whisk the mixture until it stiffens and begins to stick to the back of the spoon.

2 Gently fold in the mustard and stir until you have a deliciously smooth sauce. Serve with medallions of pork, grilled gammon or fillets of fresh cod.

SERVES 4

Right Accept no imitations!

COLD TRUTH

Whilst doctors will tell you that there is no cure for the viral common cold, it hasn't stopped people trying to ward it away with a bizzare concoction of passed-down remedies. Old wives' tales include numerous strange remedies for fighting off symptoms, from wrapping up in a red blanket to tying sweaty socks around the neck! All to little avail, though. Colds can come about as a result of the nose becoming infected by any one of 200 different individual viruses. The average cough can unleash a charge of air at 60mph; a sneeze can top the 100mph mark!

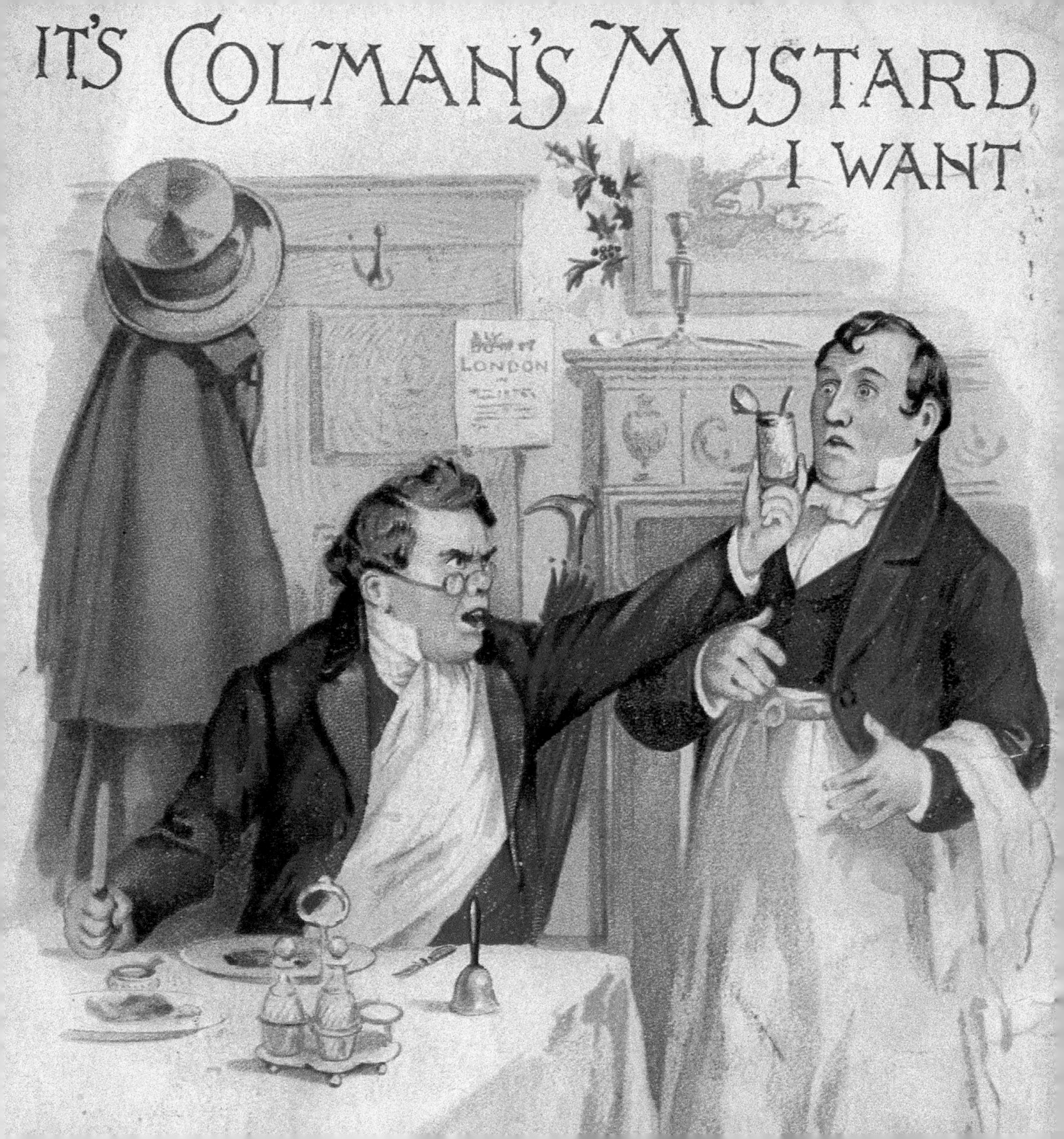
IT'S COLMAN'S MUSTARD
I WANT
LONDON

Greek-style Beetroot

4 medium-sized beetroot, cooked and still warm (this will give the best results)
110ml Greek style thick yoghurt
1 teaspoon Colman's English mustard
Pinch paprika
Warmed pitta bread to accompany

1 Slice the beetroot into rounds and arrange on a serving plate. Beat the yoghurt in a separate bowl and when smooth and creamy mix in the Colman's mustard thoroughly.

2 In one swift movement, tip the yoghurt into the centre of the arranged beetroot, garnish with a pinch of paprika and serve immediately with warm slithers of pitta bread and a bottle of crisp, well-chilled dry white wine. This dish makes a great starter on a warm summer's night.

SERVES 2

HOT FACT

Löyly (pronounced *leuw-luw*) is a Finnish word used to describe the steam that rises from hot stones. The Finns began their hot-stone-water-vaporising antics back in ancient times, when they lived in dwellings little short of mud bunkers covered over with turf. Hot stones would surround the hearth of their fireplaces, storing heat during the day, enabling the abode to stay warm through the night, without the need to tend a fire. A freaky splish-splash of water later and the Finns discovered that the stones let off even more heat when they came into contact with liquid. Voila! The sauna was invented.

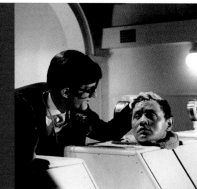

Somerset-style Pork Chops

Oil
2 pork chops
1 wine glass medium Somerset
 cider
55ml thick double cream
1 teaspoon onion marmalade,
 home-made or bought
1 teaspoon Colman's English
 mustard

1 Heat a heavy-based frying pan over a high heat, add the oil and seal the pork chops. Now lower the heat and continue until the meat is cooked just right.

2 Remove the chops from the pan and keep warm. De-glaze the pan with half of the cider and simmer to reduce the liquid to a quarter. Now add the cream, the onion marmalade and the mustard and heat through until the sauce begins to just tremble.

3 Carefully place the pork chops onto serving plates and pour over the sauce. Garnish with halved cherry tomatoes and watercress and serve with baby new potatoes and baked apples, and your remaining half-glass of cider.

SERVES 2

The Countryman's Piccalilli

3kg prepared vegetables, as follows

1 cucumber – leave skin on and cut ends off, cut into quarters and then into 2.5cm lengths

1 kg cauliflower, broken into florets, halved or quartered according to size

1 kg small shallots

500g runner beans, cut into 2.5cm slices

2 tablespoons salt

1$\frac{1}{2}$ litres malt vinegar

1 tablespoon turmeric

1 tablespoon ground ginger

1 tablespoon Colman's English mustard

2 cloves garlic, crushed

200g sugar

3 tablespoons cornflour

Salt and freshly ground black pepper

This recipe comes from Tony, a man with a passion for the countryside equal to my passion for food.

1 Place all the vegetables into a large pan, sprinkle with the salt, cover and leave overnight. The next day, drain the vegetables and rinse with cold water.

2 Put most of the vinegar into a large pan, add the spices, mustard, garlic and sugar and bring to the boil.

3 Add the vegetables, and simmer for a maximum of 3 minutes. Blend the cornflour with the remaining vinegar and stir into the mix. Boil for 2 minutes, stirring gently. Ladle into sterilised kilner jars.

MAKES APPROX. 4KG OF PICCALILLI

Sweet Potato & Mustard Mash

2 large sweet potatoes
110ml double cream
3 level teaspoons Colman's
  English mustard
Juice 1 lemon

1 First peel the sweet potatoes and cut them into large cubes. Boil them for 10 minutes in salted water until they are just tender but not soft. Drain, and transfer to a blender and add the cream. Zap for about 30 seconds until you have a smooth mixture.

2 Return the potatoes to the pan and stir in the mustard, warm through and add the lemon juice. This mash makes the perfect accompaniment to grilled gammon or fish cakes. You can serve this onto the plate by filling a well-greased large biscuit cutter and then gently removing it to leave behind a perfect mound of fantastic mash.

SERVES 4

COLD TRUTH

Stories of yetis are linked with the snow-capped mountains of the Himalayas, but this myth exists in various forms in places far and wide across the world. The Himalayan-named yeti was dubbed as such by the native Sherpa people, with yeti translating as 'dweller among the rocks'. The Chinese, though, have their very own yeti: the 'Chi-Chi' or 'Chang Mi' (wild man), whilst natives of Canada and the United States tell stories of 'Sasquatch', (or 'hairy man of the forest' – but better know as 'Bigfoot').

Cheddar Scones with Trout Pâté

225g self-raising flour
1 heaped teaspoon Colman's
  English mustard powder
Pinch salt
$1/2$ teaspoon of baking powder
40g unsalted butter
60g Cheddar cheese, grated
2 medium free-range eggs
Milk, for the glaze
150ml sour cream
Pinch cayenne pepper
100g smoked trout paté
  (either best shop-bought or
  home-made)
Lemon mayonnaise, to serve
Parsley, chopped, to serve

1 Sift the flour, mustard powder, salt and baking powder into a bowl. Using the back of a wooden spoon rub in the butter until the mixture resembles breadcrumbs. Stir in the cheese and break in one of the eggs, adding enough sour cream to form a light dough.

2 On a lightly floured surface, roll out the dough to a thickness of about 2cm and, using a traditional pastry cutter, cut out as many scones as you can, reforming the dough and rolling out again, disregarding the last bits. Place the scones onto a greased baking sheet. Beat the remaining egg with a little milk and brush the tops of the scones, finishing with a sprinkle of cayenne pepper.

3 Bake at 220C/425F/Gas 7 for about 10 minutes until golden brown. Allow to cool slightly before cutting in half, on the bias, and filling with the trout paté. Serve warm with the lemon mayonnaise and a flourish of chopped parsley.

**MAKES ABOUT
16 SMALL SCONES**

Right The bull's head of the Colman's logo was adopted as the firm's trademark in 1855. Royal approval came about ten years later vis-a-vis a warrant as manufacturers to Her Majesty Queen Victoria.

TAKE NOTICE

COLMAN'S
BEST QUALITY
MUSTARD

IS PACKED IN
1lb. ½lb. & ¼lb. TINS
OF THIS SHAPE ONLY.

TRADE MARK — BULL'S HEAD.

J. & J. COLMAN

MUSTARD MANUFACTURERS
TO THE
QUEEN.

108, CANNON STREET, LONDON.

Baked Field Mushrooms with Mustard & Tarragon Butter

6 large field mushrooms, skins peeled

For the Tarragon Butter
200g unsalted butter
2 heaped tablespoons of ready-made Colman's English mustard
1 clove garlic, peeled and mashed
1 heaped tablespoon picked leaves tarragon, roughly chopped
Juice 1 lime
Olive oil
Salt and freshly ground pepper

1 To make the tarragon butter, gently soften the butter and place in a bowl with the well-mashed garlic. Add the tarragon and the mustard, salt and pepper (but not too much as it will drown the sweet tarragon flavour). Finally, add the lime juice and mix carefully into a thick paste.

2 Pre-heat the oven to 200C/400F/Gas 6.

3 Remove the stalks from the mushrooms and place in a roasting tray. Fill the centre of each mushroom with the tarragon mustard butter. To help the cooking process its worth brushing the filled mushrooms with a little olive oil. Place the mushrooms in the oven and bake for 30 minutes. Serve on a bed of diced crispy lettuce or fresh spinach leaves drizzled with a little chilli oil.

SERVES 6

Sowing the seeds...

■■■ Mustard comes from the seeds of the mustard plant; the brown mustard plant (Brassica Juncea) produces the flour which provides the heat, whilst the white mustard plant (Sinapis Alba) produces the flour which provides the flavour. The two flours are mixed into a special Colman's recipe.

■■■ For many centuries, mustard seeds were used widely as a condiment at meal times. Before the eighteenth century, however, diners were expected to crush the seeds for themselves (in similar fashion to the way we grind pepper at the table today), some choosing to mix them with vinegar and water before flavouring their food.

Sumptuous Vinaigrette

4 x fresh raspberries
1 teaspoon runny honey
1 teaspoon red pesto
1 teaspoon ready made Colman's
   English mustard
1 level teaspoon Colman's English
   mustard powder
1 clove fresh garlic, crushed
1/2 teaspoon Lea & Perrins
   Worcestershire sauce
Freshly ground black pepper
Pinch sea salt
9 tablespoons garlic and rosemary
   oil or similar herb-infused olive oil
5 tablespoons white wine vinegar
1 dessertspoon sun-blushed
   tomatoes, chopped

1 Push the raspberries through a fine sieve with the back of a spoon to extract maximum juice and flavour. Pour the juice into a blender.

2 Add all the remaining ingredients (apart from the salt) and blitz for 40-60 seconds (or until the ingredients are blended). Add the salt and blitz again for no more than 5 seconds.

3 Pour the vinaigrette into a suitable jar or bottle ready to drizzle on your salad. It can be kept in a cool place for up to a month. Shake well before use.

MAKES APPROX. 250ML

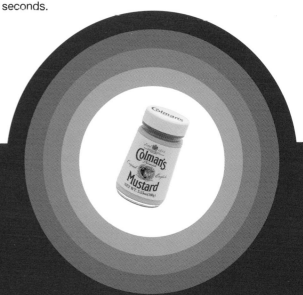

■■■ In 1720, Mrs Clements of Durham spotted that she could take the strain out of all this meal-time pestle-and-mortar action, deciding that she would grind and sift the seed before it reached the table. This new mustard 'flour' was sold as Durham Mustard and became a favourite condiment of King George I.

Devilled Chicken Drumsticks

4 teaspoons Colman's English
   mustard powder
1 dessertspoon white wine
Pinch soft brown sugar
Pinch nutmeg
1 sprig rosemary, finely chopped
   with all the stalks removed
1 dessertspoon cold water
8 chicken drumsticks, preferably
   free-range

**My mother used to make these
as a post Christmas treat using
the big turkey drumsticks**

1 Mix together in a bowl the
mustard, the wine, brown
sugar, nutmeg and chopped
rosemary, adding the water
until you have a thick
workable smooth paste.

2 Take each drumstick in turn
and make 2 or 3 incisions
into the fleshly part. Prize
them open and stuff with the
fiery yellow paste. Pull the
skin or flesh together on the
outside and tightly wrap in
kitchen foil.

3 Cook on a baking tray or in a
roasting dish in a pre-heated
oven at 180C /350F/Gas 4
for 20 minutes. Then open up
the foil parcels for a further
10 minutes to brown. Then
lift each one out of the dish
and unwrap the kitchen foil.
Now prepare a big round
plate with a covering of
diced lettuce, and place the
drumsticks with the narrow
end at the centre in a circle
(like the face of a clock).

Serve with freshly made
parsnip crisps.

SERVES 4

*Right This intrepid explorer
is headed for Klondike, the
hostile and remote Alaskan
town to where, in 1897 and
1898, 100,000 'stampeders'
were said to have set off for,
after the discovery of gold
in 1896. San Francisco
and Seattle newspapers
carried headlines of
'GOLD! GOLD! GOLD! GOLD!'
when they got wind of the
story the following year
(the news took this long
to reach the US due to the
dividing Yukon River freezing
over, thus preventing
communication.) As with
Scott's Antarctica trip,
Colman's seemed to be
a warming staple to take
for such a cruel journey.
Only four in ten men returned
alive (most without having
found a speck of gold.)*

Cod with Mustard Crust

4 x 150g cod steaks with the skin on
2 dessertspoons capers, rinsed
and chopped
3 level tablespoons of breadcrumbs
100g Parmesan
2 tablespoons Colman's English
mustard powder
1 heaped tablespoon chopped
fresh mint
Salt and freshly ground black pepper
25g butter
1 dessertspoon vegetable oil
1 tablespoon chopped fresh parsley
Zest 1 lemon

1 In a heavy-based frying pan heat the butter and oil over a high heat. Fry the cod steaks skin-side down only – do not turn them over. When the skin is good and crispy take the steaks from the frying pan and leave to cool.

2 Make the crust: in a bowl mix the breadcrumbs, Parmesan, mustard, salt and pepper and chopped mint. This can be made in advance and kept cool in the fridge.

3 With all the ingredients at room temperature, press the crust mixture on top of the cod steak – skin-side up.

4 Pre-heat the oven to 200C/400F/Gas 6 and cook the crusted cod steaks for 8 minutes. Remove them from the pan and let them rest for another 3 minutes before sprinkling with the parsley and lemon zest. Serve with lemon couscous, crunchy mangetout and a chilled, flinty Muscadet de Sevre et Maine sur Lie.

SERVES 4

Right '*Returned from Klondyke': One of the lucky few who did!*

COLMAN'S MUSTARD

"Returned from Klondyke"

Broccoli & Stilton Quiche

250g short crust pastry
Small knob butter
200g finely chopped onions
1 red pepper
1 dessertspoon Demerara sugar
2 dessertspoons Colman's English
    mustard powder
200g broccoli florets, blanched
200g Stilton, crumbled
6 large eggs, beaten

You will need a 10-inch flan dish.

1 Pre-heat the oven 220C/425F/Gas 7. Roll out the pastry, and line the flan dish with it. Place in the fridge for 30 minutes. Prick the base with a fork then line with baking parchment, fill with baking beans and bake blind in the pre-heated oven for 10 minutes.

2 Remove the flan dish and reduce the oven temperature to 180C/350F/Gas 4.

3 Melt the butter in a frying pan and add the onions.

Gently fry the onions until they start to colour. Add the red pepper, sugar and mustard and continue to fry gently for a couple of minutes more. Spread the onion mixture over the baked flan base and arrange the broccoli florets on top. Add the Stilton and the beaten eggs. Carefully return the flan dish to the oven, and bake for a further 20 minutes. To test if your quiche is cooked, pierce with a fork – it should come out clean.

SERVES 6-8

Parma Ham and Asparagus with Fig & Port Mustard

8 slices Parma ham
8 spears freshly cooked asparagus
250g fresh figs, peeled and quartered
150ml port
1 dessertspoon Colman's English mustard
$\frac{1}{2}$ teaspoon caster sugar

1 Take 4 wafer thin slices of Parma ham per person and lay them out flat. Place one piece of asparagus at one end and roll up into a cylinder making sure that the asparagus spear peeps out of one end. Repeat for all 8 slices.

2 Drop the fresh figs, port, Colman's mustard and sugar into a blender and blitz for 20 seconds.

3 Place the rolled Parma ham and asparagus on a plate and drizzle with the sauce.

SERVES 2 AS A STARTER

Great Scott!...

■■■ *'I have much pleasure in informing you that the flour, cornflour and mustard supplied by you to this expedition has proven entirely satisfactory. I have to especially thank you for the careful manner in which your food was packed.'*
Letter from Captain Scott, on his second Antarctica trek, to J.J. Colman, Carrow Works, Norwich.

Colman's Scotch Eggs

400g sausage meat
150g prepared sage and onion
   stuffing mix
1 tablespoon Colman's English
   mustard
Salt and ground black pepper
8 large free-range eggs,
   hard-boiled
2 medium free-range eggs
1/2 teaspoon Colman's English
   mustard powder
200g fresh breadcrumbs
Vegetable oil for deep-frying

1 Mix together the sausage meat, the sage and onion stuffing mix (made as per the instructions on the packet) and the mustard. Season with salt and pepper and then divide the mixture into 8 equal portions.

2 Cut 8 pieces of clingfilm, each approximately 15cm square. Spread out the sausage meat mix on each piece, lay the egg in the centre and gather up the clingfilm, moulding the sausage meat inside around the egg until it is completely covered, leaving the clingfilm on. Repeat until all the eggs are coated and chill in the fridge for 2-3 hours. Remove clingfilm.

3 In a small bowl beat the raw egg and the mustard powder. In a second dish, lay out the breadcrumbs. Now roll the sausage-meat-covered eggs firstly in the egg and mustard mix and then in the breadcrumbs, taking care to completely coat them during both actions. When all the eggs have been covered, place them in the fridge for 2-3 hours. This will set the coating and ensure that it doesn't fall off during cooking.

4 If you have a deep fat fryer, set it to 190C/375F, or alternatively pour about 7.5cm of vegetable oil into a heavy-based saucepan and heat until just smoking. Fry 2-3 eggs in the hot fat at the same time. When the coating has turned golden brown, remove from the hot oil and drain on kitchen paper. Serve cut in half, with chunks of cheese and fresh tomatoes and a good dollop of Colman's English mustard!

MAKES 8 EGGS

Sherried Rabbit with Rustic Vegetables

1 tablespoon olive oil
1 large onion, roughly chopped
1 large carrot, roughly chopped
2 sticks celery, sliced
1 large clove garlic, finely sliced
1 whole rabbit
3-4 peppercorns
Good pinch salt
1 tablespoon plain flour
1 tablespoon Colman's English
   mustard powder
500ml dry sherry
2 tablespoons parsley, freshly
   chopped
2 bay leaves

1 Pre-heat the oven to 170C/ 325F/Gas 3. Place a deep frying pan on a medium to high hob, pour in the olive oil and add the onions, carrots, celery and garlic and fry gently until starting to colour.

2 Now place the rabbit on top of the vegetables and continue to fry for approximately 5-10 minutes, turning the rabbit regularly to get a good colouring all over. Add the peppercorns and season with salt. Blend the flour, mustard powder and sherry until you have a paste, then gradually stir it into the juices in the pan.

3 Transfer to a baking dish, adding the parsley and bay leaves, and cook for a couple of hours until the meat separates easily from the carcass. Lovely served with Sweet Potato & Mustard Mash (see p19) and a glass of chilled Fino.

SERVES 2

HOT FACT

Our fascination with flame began over $1^{1}/_{2}$ million years ago. The evolution of the humble matchstick begins in pre-history, when cavemen rubbed two pieces of wood together. This basic concept – one surface abrading against another – took focused form in the 17th century with the discovery of phosphorous. A few years later saw Robert Boyle experimenting with phosphorous-coated paper and sulphur-coated wooden splints. It was in 1826 that John Walker chanced upon the matchstick proper (scraping a mixture-coated stick across his floor). But it was Samuel Jones who sprang to patent the idea and, in no time at all, 'Lucifer's' matches hit the shops!

Giant's Canapés

2 tablespoons runny honey
1 tablespoon Colman's English
   mustard powder
Juice $\frac{1}{2}$ a lemon
6 best-quality sausages

1 Mix together the honey, mustard powder and lemon juice and with a pastry brush coat the sausages all over and then bake them in a pre-heated oven at 200C/ 400F/ Gas 6 for 20 minutes.

2 When the sausages are cooked, display on a big round white plate with a white (yes it must be white) bowl in the centre. While the sausages were cooking, prepare some standard mashed potato and using the handle of a wooden spoon swirl in 3 teaspoons of green pesto. Your guests can then dip the mustardy bangers into the pesto mash.

SERVES 4

Strange sayings...

■■■ *To cut the mustard.*
To succeed, to have the ability to do what's necessary. 'He didn't cut much mustard' is an American phrase that dates back to about 1900. Mustard was a slang variant for 'real thing' or 'genuine article', and this may have contributed to the idiom.

But, also, mustard is a very difficult crop to harvest, so not being able to 'cut it' could similarly suggest that you don't have what's required. To *cut the muster*, meanwhile, means to be 'well turned out'. It's conceivable that 'cut the mustard' could have come about as a botched translation of this saying.

Spinach, Mushroom and Chorizo Salad

300g freshly washed raw spinach, torn into bite-size pieces
100g button mushrooms, sliced
25g butter
1 clove garlic, finely chopped
2 Spanish chorizo sausages, sliced into 1.5cm rings

For the dressing
9 teaspoons good olive oil
5 teaspoons tarragon vinegar
Pinch salt
Freshly ground black pepper
1 teaspoon Colman's English mustard powder

1 Toss the spinach into a salad bowl and sprinkle with the raw sliced mushroom and set aside.

2 In a frying pan, melt the butter and gently fry the garlic for about 4-5 minutes. Add the chorizo, and fry for about 3 minutes to warm through.

3 Meanwhile, place all the dressing ingredients into a blender and blitz for 20 seconds. Take the chorizo from the frying pan and drain on

kitchen paper before sprinkling it over the salad. Drizzle with the dressing and serve with chunks of bread.

SERVES 2

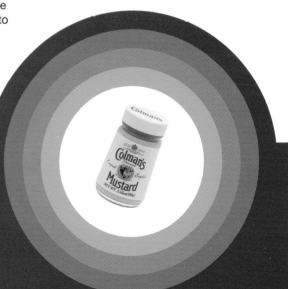

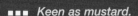 *Keen as mustard.*
To be very sharp, extremely keen. Thomas Keen's company made mustard from 1742 until 1903, when the business was acquired by Colman's. Keen is often associated with the origins of the phrase, but the phrase 'the keenest mustard' pre-dates Keen by almost 100 years.

Mussel Power

1kg frozen green-lip mussels
   in their half shell
Colman's English mustard
1 tube tomato purée
2 large cloves garlic, finely
   chopped
Fresh white breadcrumbs
Olive oil
Parsley, to garnish

1 Defrost the mussels in their shells, then drain and pat dry. Coat the flesh of each mussel with a thin spread of Colman's English mustard followed by a small dollop of tomato purée straight from the tube and spread over.

2 Sprinkle all the chopped garlic over the coated mussels and then cover with breadcrumbs. Lay out the mussels in a shallow roasting tin and drizzle lightly with olive oil.

3 Place under a medium hot grill for 3-4 minutes until the breadcrumbs are toasted to golden. Scatter with fresh parsley and a good grind of black pepper. Serve as tapas with chilled Cava or other decent-quality fizz, or just as a great lunch with plenty of warm crusty bread.

SERVES 4-6

Right 'The Mustard Club' was a famous advertising campaign that ran from 1926 to 1933. The club comprised a playfully quaint coterie of individuals, such as Master Mustard, Signor de Spaghetti and the club's president, Baron de Beef. Artists William Brearley and John Gilroy, and copywriters Dorothy L. Sayers and Oswald Green were the geniuses who created the cartoons that decorated magazines and many billboards of the day.

THE ADVENTURES OF THE MUSTARD CLUB

Being a selection of the famous advertisements of the MUSTARD CLUB, together with many interesting cartoons and hitherto unpublished documents.

PRICE
6D.

Stuffed Peppers with Brie and Mustard

4 red peppers
25g butter
1 medium-sized red onion, roughly
    chopped
2 small leeks, sliced
150g cup mushrooms, sliced
1 dessertspoon Colman's English
    mustard
Small glass white wine
100g Somerset Brie, cut into small
    pieces, rind on
Salt and black pepper

1 Halve the peppers lengthways and remove the seeds – you may leave the stalk in for decoration. Place the peppers in boiling water for about $1^{1}/_{2}$ minutes, remove and chill quickly in cold water (preferably iced). Place the pepper on some kitchen paper to dry whilst you are preparing the filling.

2 Melt the butter in a pan and add the onions and leeks and cook on a low heat for about 3-4 minutes. Add the mushrooms, mustard, wine and bring to the boil. Cook until the liquid has reduced by half. Remove from the heat, stir in the Brie and then fill the peppers with the mixture. The peppers can be served warm or cold. To serve warm, simply place on an oven tray and gently warm in the oven at 150C/300F/Gas 2 for about 10 minutes. Great with salad, vegetables or sauté potatoes.

SERVES 2

Right Another member for The Mustard Club!

Fillet of Beef Romanoff

1 tablespoon olive oil
1 medium-sized onion, finely
    chopped
750g fillet of beef cut into
    5cm x 1cm strips (ask your
    butcher for tail end of fillets)
1 large pickled dill, roughly
    chopped
100g closed-cup mushrooms,
    sliced
3 heaped teaspoons Colman's
    English mustard
Salt and ground black pepper
1 large glass red wine

1 Heat the wok on the stove with the olive oil in it. Drop in the onions and cook for 2 minutes, then add the sliced mushrooms and cook for a further 2 minutes

2 Next add the cracked pepper, mustard, chopped dill and the wine and stir well. Turn up the heat to reduce the liquid and then add the beef to the sizzling juices. Cook for a further 2-3 minutes until the beef is glossy but still rare and ready to be devoured.

SERVES 4

*Right and below
The club's President,
Baron de Beef.*

MUSTERING OF THE MUSTARD CLUB

Mustard Cheese Straws

100g ready-made puff pastry
2 heaped teaspoons Colman's
  English mustard
50g mature farmhouse Cheddar,
  grated
1 teaspoon fresh parsley, finely
  chopped

1 Pre-heat the oven to 190C/ 375F/Gas 5. Roll the pastry on a floured board until 3-4mm thick. Spread the mustard over the pastry, then sprinkle the cheese over evenly and scatter the parsley on top. Cover with clingfilm, press down firmly and chill for 30 minutes. This will make it easier to cut as well as producing good pastry.

2 Remove the pastry from the fridge and cut into 7.5 x 1cm strips. Place the strips on a greased baking tray with space between to expand during cooking.

3 Place the tray in the top of the oven for 10-15 minutes or until the cheese straws have risen and the cheese looks crisp on the outside. Leave to cool slightly, and then arrange on a plate ready for cocktails at 6.

MAKES 16

Quick tips...

■■■ To remove odours such as fish or garlic from dishes and utensils, add a tablespoon of Colman's English mustard to your washing-up water to help remove the whiff!

■■■ Similarly, if your hands smell of onions or spice, try rubbing some Colman's English mustard onto them, before rinsing with warm water, and this should diminish the odour.

Stir-fried Monkfish

25g butter
1 small onion, finely diced
1 tablespoon prepared Colman's
 English mustard
500g trimmed and filleted
 monkfish, diced into 3cm chunks
50ml Scotch whisky
2 tomatoes, skinned, de-seeded
 and diced
Juice 1 lemon
Salt and pepper, to season
1 small wine glass cream sherry
150ml double cream
1 teaspoon tomato purée

1 Place a wok over a medium heat and add the butter and finely diced onion and stir-fry until softened – do not let the onions colour. Add the mustard, mix well and cook gently for 2-3 minutes. With lighter in hand, pour in the whisky and ignite it, being careful to ensure eyebrows and hair are well out of the way.

2 Add the tomato, lemon juice a sprinkling of salt and the sherry. Mix well, and now reduce the liquid over a high heat for 3-4 minutes. Turn down the heat, add the cream and the tomato purée and simmer gently for 10 minutes. Finally, add the monkfish and cook for a further 3-4 minutes so that it is just cooked. Serve with a crispy, lightly dressed endive salad.

SERVES 2

■■■ Blocked nose or sore throat? Try smearing a bit of Colman's English mustard over a slice of bread or savoury biscuit. Research has shown that hot or spicy foodstuffs stimulate the secretion of mucus in the airway, which helps to soothe and relieve the congestion of the nose and throat.

Classic Colman's Cheese Sauce

500ml double cream
1 level tablespoon Colman's
  English mustard
200g Cheddar, grated
Salt

1 Bring the cream and the mustard to a rolling boil in a small saucepan, whisking all the time – do not allow to boil over. As the mixture starts to just boil, add the grated cheese. Now turn down the heat a little and allow the cheese to melt into the mixture.

2 When all the cheese has melted you will have a wonderful sauce that is naturally thickened. Add salt to taste and finally a further splash more of mustard for a real 'cheese twist'.

MAKES APPROX. 600ML

COLD TRUTH

Did you know that eskimos have more than thirty common ways of describing snow? These account for the myriad nuances of snow and the way that it falls and spreads. *Apun* is simply 'snow' and *kannik* is 'snowflake'; but there are words and word-units for drifting snow, for newly drifted snow, for the rippled surface of snow, even for snow which settles on clothes. *Sisuuk* means 'avalanche'.

Colman's-style Baked Chicken Kiev

For the filling
125g Ricotta cheese
100g butter, softened
Zest and juice 1 lime
2 cloves garlic, finely chopped
1 heaped teaspoon Colman's
   mustard powder
1 dessertspoon finely chopped
   parsley
Salt and pepper

4 Chicken breasts

For the coating
250g breadcrumbs
1 medium free-range egg whisked
   with 100ml milk
About 50g plain flour

**Ask your butcher to remove
the skin off the chicken breasts,
trim the wing bone and leave in,
and cut the chicken to make it
easy for stuffing.**

1 In a small bowl, mix together all the ingredients for the filling. Place the chicken breasts on a board and open them out. Divide the mixture from the small bowl into 4 equal parts. Place a spoon of mixture just under the knuckle of the bone so as to sit it in the centre of the chicken breast. Fold all the sides of the chicken breast over the mixture to ensure the mixture is completely wrapped. Repeat with the remaining chicken breasts.

2 Take each filled breast and dust lightly with the flour and dip each one into the beaten egg and milk. Finally, roll carefully in the breadcrumbs, then back into the egg and milk and again roll in the breadcrumbs.

3 Pre-heat the oven to 180C/350F/Gas 4. Place the chicken breasts on a greased baking tray and bake for 30 minutes. Remove and rest the chicken for 5 minutes. Serve with sauté potatoes or Fennel Coleslaw with Mustard Mayo (see p13).

SERVES 4

Stuffed Mushrooms

450g medium-sized cup
   mushrooms
100g butter
1 medium onion, roughly chopped
3 gloves garlic, roughly chopped
1 tablespoons Colman's English
   mustard powder
2 tablespoons chopped chives
Salt and pepper
1 lemon (half for juice and half for
   the garnish)
3 slices wholemeal bread

1 Remove the stalks from the mushrooms carefully, so that you don't split them. A little pressure on the stalk from side to side should suffice. Chop the stalks and set aside.

2 Melt the butter in a saucepan over a low to medium heat and add the whole de-stalked mushrooms, stir, coating the mushrooms with the butter. Remove and set aside.
In the same pan place the onion, garlic, mushroom stalks and gently cook for 4-5 minutes until the onions have softened. Add the mustard, chives and season with salt and pepper and the juice from half the lemon. Stir and remove from the heat.

3 In a blender, place the bread and the onion and mustard mixture and zap the lot together. With a teaspoon, fill the mushroom cups and place filled side up on a baking tray. Before serving, bake in a pre-heated oven at 180C/350F/Gas 4 for about 10 minutes. Serve the mushrooms on a bed of shredded lettuce with a dollop of garlic mayonnaise.

**SERVES 6
AS A STARTER**

*Right What better
reminder of home?*

Spaghetti Royale

500g spaghetti
25g butter
1 level teaspoon Colman's English
  mustard powder
Freshly ground black pepper
1 tablespoon chopped flat-leaf
  parsley
Parmesan, freshly grated

1 Cook the spaghetti in boiling water until just al dente and drain in a colander.

2 Return the drained pasta to the hot pan, add the butter and the mustard, a good grind of black pepper and the flat-leaf parsley. Mix together well and serve.

3 Have a bowl of freshly grated Parmesan on the table and serve with a fresh and vibrant tomato and basil salad.

SERVES 4

Mustard and the Bard...

■■■ Mustard-Seed was one of the fairies who beckoned to the calls of Titiana, the Fairy Queen in *A Midsummer Night's Dream*.

■■■ 'What say you to a piece of beef and mustard?'
Grumio to Katharina, *The Taming of the Shrew*

■■■ 'Of a certain knight that swore by his honour they were good pancakes and swore by his honour the mustard was naught[...]'
Touchstone to Celia, *As You Like It*

■■■ 'His wits as thick as Tewkesbury Mustard.'
Henry IV Part II

Smoked Salmon with Sweet Mustard Sauce

12 slices Scottish smoked salmon

For the sauce
1 large free-range egg (yolk only)
2 tablespoons Colman's English mustard
1 tablespoon soft brown sugar
1 tablespoon Mascarpone cheese
6 tablespoons olive oil
2 tablespoons cider vinegar
2 tablespoons fresh dill. finely chopped
4 pieces fresh dill left whole, for the garnish
1 lime cut into 8 segments
Toasted fingers of brown bread, to accompany

1 In a food processor or blender drop in the egg yolk, mustard, sugar and Mascarpone and blitz for about 10 seconds. Leaving the machine running, gently add the olive oil, the vinegar and chopped dill and within 30 seconds you should have a delicious thick sauce.

2 On each plate, place three rolls of smoked salmon (like a propeller blade) between each roll put first the lime, second the throng of fresh dill and lastly a good dollop of the sweet mustard sauce. Serve with lightly toasted fingers of brown bread.

SERVES 4

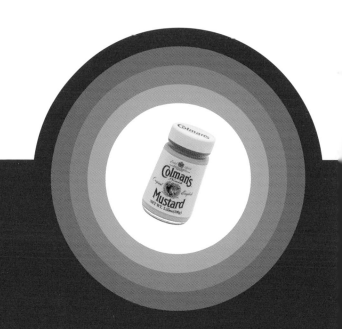

■■■ Other notable literary mentions include appearances in the writings of Anton Chekhov, Alexandre Dumas, Jerome K. Jerome and Hans Christian-Anderson.

Spiced Rarebit

50ml pineapple juice
50ml coconut milk
1 teaspoon rum essence
2 level teaspoons Colman's
   English mustard powder
$1/2$ teaspoon cayenne pepper
400g mature Cheddar, grated
6 slices of thick, toasted bread
6 good sprigs of fresh watercress
A pinch of smoked paprika
Spicy mango chutney,
   to accompany

1 In a bowl, mix the pineapple juice, coconut milk and rum essence with the mustard powder and cayenne pepper and set aside for 30 minutes. Place the mixture in a saucepan and slowly bring to the boil, adding the grated cheese a little at a time.

2 When all the cheese has melted, remove the pan from the heat and allow to cool. Toast the bread and pour the cheese mixture over the slices of toast. Place them all under a medium hot grill until the cheese begins to bubble and turn golden. Place on bright white plates with a sprig of watercress and a final pinch of smoked paprika. Accompany with mango chutney.

SERVES 6

Right Colman's English mustard: exported far and wide, all over the world.

ALL OVER THE WORLD

COLMAN'S D.S.F. MUSTARD

Hot Bratwurst with Chilli Mustard

For the Chilli Mustard

2 tablespoons Colman's English
   mustard powder
4 finely chopped red chillies,
   seeds removed
1 tablespoon soft brown sugar
25g flour
25ml white wine vinegar

8 German Bratwurst – if Bratwurst
   is unavailable, any good German
   sausage can be used
1 loaf black rye bread
$1/2$ teaspoon salt

1 To make the chilli mustard, blitz all of the ingredients together in a food blender. (For even more flavour leave for 2-3 days before using.)

2 Grill or griddle the Bratwurst quite slowly to avoid the skins splitting. In the mean time, prepare 4 plates each with 2 halves of freshly cut rye bread. When the Bratwurst is ready, place them on the plates and top with big dollops of chilli mustard.

SERVES 4

Right Ahh! The perfect setting.

Colman's
Mustard

Roast Rib of Beef with Malayan Mustard

2 kg rib of beef

For the Malayan Mustard
1 dessertspoon Colman's English mustard powder
3 teaspoons finely chopped galangal or fresh ginger
2 teaspoons crushed dried chillies
4 cloves garlic, finely chopped
Vinegar, to blend

1 Pre-heat the oven to 200C/400F/Gas 6.

2 Using a hand blender or a pestle and mortar, mix all the mustard ingredients together, gradually adding enough vinegar to create a paste. Spread this paste all over the meat and leave the rib to stand in a roasting tin for 30 minutes so that the flavours seep in.

3 Put the beef into the oven for 15 minutes and then reduce the temperature to 150C/300F/Gas 2 and cook for a further 1 hour. This will give you a crispy but rare meat in the centre. For medium beef add 15 minutes to the final cooking time and for well-done beef add a further 15 minutes.

4 When cooked to your liking, allow the beef to stand for a good 10 minutes for the meat to relax and the juices to settle back before carving. Wonderful served hot with your favourite roast vegetables or cold with salad and pickles.

SERVES 4

Peach & Asparagus Pasta Penne

1 bunch fresh asparagus
500g pasta penne
250ml crème fraîche
2 teaspoons Colman's English
  mustard
2 firm but ripe peaches, stoned
  and sliced into 8
Chopped chives, to garnish
Black pepper, freshly milled
50g Parmesan

1 Break off the woody base of the asparagus and cut the spears into 2-3cm lengths. Steam for 3-4 minutes and refresh under cold water.

2 Cook the pasta in plenty of boiling salted water until just *al dente* and then drain and return to the pan. Add the crème fraîche and mustard and toss the pasta with a slotted spoon to coat it well. Next add the asparagus and the peach slices and turn the whole mixture very gently once or twice.

3 Pour out the pasta onto 4 warmed serving plates, scatter with chopped chives and season with black pepper. A few Parmesan shavings scattered over the top will finish the dish to perfection.

SERVES 4

HOT FACT

When we overheat, we cool ourselves down by perspiring, but did you know that this simple process we take for granted can call upon the resources of over two million individual sweat glands? These sudoriferous glands secrete a mixture of water, fatty acids and minerals, and any odour is determined by the amount of bacteria that mix with these secretions. About one-eighth of these can be found in the feet, which release about eight ounces of moisture a day! The average adult loses 500-plus calories with every litre of sweat. And the sweatier sex? Men: they sweat about 40% more than women.

Spiced Dough Balls

100g butter, softened
150g mature Cheddar, grated
150g self-raising flour
1 rounded teaspoon Colman's
    mustard powder
Freshly ground black pepper
Pinch sea salt
2 medium free-range eggs, beaten

1 Beat together the softened butter and the grated cheese until well blended. Add all the dry ingredients and mix well.

2 Gradually add the eggs to form a dough and roll into marble-sized balls using floured hands. If the dough seems too wet, just add a little more flour.

3 Place on greased baking trays and bake for 10-15 minutes at 180C/350F/Gas4.

MAKES 12-18 DOUGH BALLS

Right In its glory indeed!

Salad of Smoked Duck with Mild Chilli Vinaigrette

1 Oakleaf or frisée lettuce, washed
  and leaves torn
50g sliced fresh radish
50g finely sliced red onion

For the Chilli Vinaigrette
4 tablespoons olive oil
1 tablespoon white wine vinegar
1 teaspoon Colman's English
  mustard
4 good dashes mild green
  Tabasco sauce
Juice $^1/_2$ lemon
2 teaspoons runny honey

2 smoked duck breasts
Freshly ground black pepper

1 Put the lettuce leaves, radish and onions into a bowl and combine well. In a blender, blitz the oil, vinegar, mustard, honey, Tabasco and lemon juice and pour over the salad. Toss the salad well to coat all the leaves. Pile the tossed salad onto 4 plates.

2 Slice the duck breasts very thinly and arrange over the top of each salad portion. Pour any remaining juices from the salad bowl over the duck slices and finish with a good grind of black pepper. Serve with crusty bread.

SERVES 4

Packing punch...

■■■ The heat of mustard emanates from the oils which are released when the seeds are crushed. These oils contain chemicals and enzymes which, when mixed with water, react to free compounds known as *isothiocyanates*. When mixing mustard flour with water, it can take up to about 15 minutes for the mustard to reach its most potent heat.

Chilli peppers, on the other hand, are measured in Scoville heat units. In 1912, the US pharmacist, Wilbur Scoville, devised a test which determined the amount of capsicum (the active heat element) within chillies. His scale ranges from the humble bell pepper, which rates a '0', to the fiery jalapeño pepper, which registers at about the 3,000 mark, up to the scorching

Cider-glazed Gammon Steaks

4 gammon steaks
275ml Somerset cider
1 tablespoon honey
1 dessertspoon Colman's English
  mustard
2-3 slices fresh pineapple, about
  1cm thick, cubed

1 Cut incisions into the gammon steaks around the fat side, about 5cm apart. Place them in a fairly deep baking tray. Pour over most of the cider. Drizzle with the honey. Coat the gammon steaks with the mustard by placing the mustard in a sieve and gently tapping the sides to coat evenly. Place the tray under a very hot grill and cook till everything is sizzling nicely (about 10 minutes). Remove the steaks from the tray.

2 Arrange the cooked gammons on plates and keep warm.

3 Place the cooking tray back on a high heat, adding a little more cider, and the finely cubed pineapple. Whisk the mixture together and pour back over the gammon. Serve with braised fennel and sauté potatoes.

SERVES 4

habañero pepper, which clocks in at an incredible 500,000 units! Pure capsicum measures an incredible 16,000,000 units, but a chilli would never contain anywhere near this concentration. The ribs of the chilli contain the highest level, followed by the seeds and then the flesh and skin. Colman's is hot, but not that hot!

Lord Kitchener's Mackerel

2 whole large mackerel – ask your
  fishmonger to butterfly fillet
  them
Butter to grease the cooking tray
Salt and ground black pepper
1 bunch watercress, stalks
  removed
1 tablespoon prepared Colman's
  English mustard
125ml medium white wine –
  a Chardonnay would be good
$1/2$ fish stock cube
150ml double cream
Juice 1 lemon

1 Place the mackerel fillets
skin-side down on a well-
greased baking tray, sprinkle
with salt and black pepper.
Place under a low grill for
8-10 minutes, keeping an
eye on them to ensure that
the butter doesn't burn.

2 Roughly chop half of the
watercress and set aside.
In a pan, place the mustard
and the white wine with the
stock cube added. Bring to
the boil. Add the chopped
watercress and the double
cream. Boil gently to reduce
the sauce by about half (this
should take 3-4 minutes).

3 Remove the mackerel fillets
from the cooking tray and
keep warm. Add the juice of
1 lemon to the cooking juices
and add the rest of the
watercress, just long enough
to let it wilt. Pour some of the
watercress sauce onto each
plate, place the mackerel on
top and drizzle with the
remaining sauce. Makes
a perfect light lunch served
with parsnip crisps and a
rocket salad.

SERVES 2

*Right Used and loved
by all kinds of folk!*

Sausage & Cider Hotpot

2 tablespoons olive oil
1 large red onion, roughly chopped
2 cloves garlic, finely chopped
8 pork and herb sausages
450g pork belly, rind removed and
  diced
500ml medium cider
1 vegetable bouillon cube
1 heaped teaspoon Colman's
  English mustard powder
1 teaspoon roughly picked thyme
1 teaspoon fresh sage leaves, torn
3 bay leaves
Black pepper
200g broad beans, preferably
  fresh, but frozen will be OK

1 Heat the oil in a large heavy-based frying pan and gently fry the onions and garlic for 3-4 minutes. Add the sausages and pork belly and continue cooking until just browned.

2 Transfer the sausage mixture to a large casserole dish and add the cider, crumbled stock cube, mustard and herbs. Season with black pepper. Cook in a pre-heated oven 200C/400F/Gas 6 for 30 minutes, uncovered.

3 Remove the casserole from the oven, add the broad beans and stir. Return the casserole to the oven for a further 30 minutes. When cooked remove from the oven and allow to stand for at least 5 minutes before serving. Great with Basmati rice or sweet potato chips.

SERVES 4

Apricot Mustard Grilling Sauce

2 tablespoons Colman's English
   mustard powder
1 tablespoon dried apricots, finely
   diced (Mi-Cuit dried apricots are
   very good)
1 tablespoon dry sherry
1$\frac{1}{2}$ tablespoons good quality
   apricot jam
1 dessertspoon soy sauce
Pinch saffron

1 Place all the ingredients into a blender and blitz for a 20-30 seconds until you have a good consistency sauce. Pour into a jug or jar for storage.

2 Use to brush onto meat whilst roasting (especially good on pork) or use as a sauce when barbecuing or serving cold meats, cheese or pâtés.

3 If you increase the quantities proportionately, you can make larger batches of this fantastically versatile sauce.

**MAKES APPROX.
50ML**

COLD TRUTH

The world's coldest inhabited village is Oymyakon, in Yakutia, which is in eastern Siberia. Temperatures there can plummet to an incredible -70°C. January is the coldest month, where temperatures average -50°C. The town lies in a valley surrounded either side by two high mountains that cage the cold winter air and prevent any warmer air getting in. Oymyakon is home to about 900 people. In the middle of the town, there is a monument with an inscription that reads 'Oymyakon – Poljus Holoda', which translates as Oymyakon, Pole of Cold.

Leek & Mustard Crumble

1 kg baby leeks, trimmed and cut into 5cm lengths
25g butter
50g plain flour
200ml warm milk
150g Cheddar cheese, grated
25g Parmesan cheese, grated
2 teaspoons Colman's English mustard
Salt and black pepper

For the crumble
4 tablespoons fresh white breadcrumbs
25g Cheddar cheese, grated
1 tablespoon parsley, chopped

1 Pre-heat the oven to 200C/400F/Gas 6. Bring the leeks to the boil in a pan of salted water and simmer for 3 minutes. Remove from the heat, drain and plunge into cold water. Set aside.

2 In a small saucepan, melt the butter and then add the flour, stirring constantly for 2 minutes. Gradually add the warm milk until the mixture re-heats and thickens. Reduce the heat and add the grated Cheddar and Parmesan, stirring as you add. Lastly add the mustard and season with a little salt and freshly ground black pepper.

3 Put the leeks into a shallow ovenproof dish and pour the cheese sauce over the top. Sprinkle with the breadcrumbs and top with grated Cheddar cheese and parsley. Bake in the oven for about 20 minutes until the crumbs on top have turned to a golden brown. Leave to cool a little before serving.

SERVES 4

Mustard most odd...

■■■ The Mount Horeb Mustard Museum in Wisconsin, USA is home to the world's largest individual collection of mustards and mustard memorabilia – more than 4,000 different pots and jars. Curator Barry Levenson has been collecting mustard since 1986, and his range just keeps growing!

■■■ What links mustard with billiard rooms and candlesticks? Why the board game, Cluedo! Colonel Mustard is one of the six characters from the boardgame that was dreamed up by Birmingham solicitor's clerk Anthony Pratt and his wife, and released by Waddingtons in 1948.

Chive & Mustard Bread

100g unsalted butter, softened
2 teaspoons ready-made Colman's
   English mustard
1 level dessertspoon finely
   chopped chives
1 x French bread stick

1 Pre-heat the oven to 200C/400F/Gas6. Mix together the butter, mustard and the chives. Cut the French stick every 20ml, almost right through but not quite. Carefully prize each cut piece open and coat both sides with the mustard and chive butter.

2 Wrap the whole bread stick in foil, place on a roasting tray and bake in the pre-heated oven for 20 minutes, opening up the foil for the last 5 minutes to crisp up the top crust. Serve straight from the foil in the centre of your table so that everyone can rip off a chunk!

MAKES 1 LOAF

■■■ A 'mustard-chucker' is an archaic term for a pickpocket. It was used to describe street criminals who would temporarily blind their victims by throwing (mustard) powder into their faces, before looting their pockets.

MEAT *needs*

MUSTARD

COLMAN'S MUSTARD: A HEATED HISTORY

(AND OTHER YELLOW TANGENTS)

In 1814, an advertisement appeared in the Norfolk Chronicle:

'Jeremiah Colman, having taken the Stock and Trade lately carried on by Mr Edward Ames, respectfully informs his customers and the public in general that he will continue the manufacturing of Mustard'

1823

Jeremiah Colman takes his adopted nephew, James, into partnership in his new firm and calls it J & J Colman. Together they establish 'Stoke Mill', four miles south of Norwich – to become their business premises for many years.

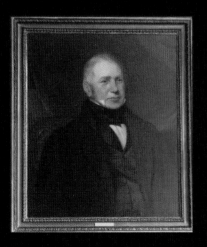

1826

As yellow fever of a sort grips a mustard-crazy Norfolk, UK, yellow fever of the worst kind is ravaging Norfolk, Virginia in the US. The plague has already visited this city three times before, in 1795, 1802 and 1821. Tragically, Norfolk would experience its worst outbreak almost a quarter of a century later, when two thousand would fall to the epidemic.

1836

Colman's almost double in size and, as a result, a branch is set up in London's Cannon Street.

1851

Jeremiah James became a partner of the firm after the death of his great uncle Jeremiah.

1854

After the death of his father, Jeremiah James is left in sole charge of the business.

1855

The now-famous bull's head logo begins to appear on the company's mustard products and is introduced as the firm's trademark.

1855

The Treskilling Yellow Swedish postage stamp is issued. It's the only one of its kind in the world (it's been printed in the wrong colour; all of the others are green), and it will change hands many times before it reaches a valuation of $2.3 million almost 150 years later.

1857

Colman's pioneering achievements in social welfare date from this period. It begins with the establishment of a school in Norwich for the children of employees at the Carrow premises.

1866

The ultimate seal of approval: the company is granted the Royal Warrant as manufacturers to Queen Victoria.

1868

Mrs Colman initiated a hot meal at lunchtime for the employees, another pioneering idea that contributed to the social welfare of the workforce.

1872

The world's first national park, Yellowstone National Park, is established by President Ulysses Grant on March 1st. Over 2.2 million acres of wilderness is to be 'set apart as a public park or pleasuring ground for the benefit and enjoyment of the people'.

1880

Handsome pictorial tins were first issued, as was the popular Penny Oval mustard tin.

1893

The *New York World* becomes the first newspaper to embellish their pages with an additional colour (yellow).

1896

The world's first cartoon strip, 'The Yellow Kid', is published in the *New York Journal* on October 18th. The Yellow Kid was first called Mickey Dugan – a bald, flap-eared, shy man who spoke via the words inscribed on his yellow nightshirt, often to make fun of upper-class customs.

1898

Jeremiah James dies. His funeral sees the whole of Norwich come to a standstill, as people mourn the passing of the son who has turned the city into a thriving manufacturing centre.

1903

A rival mustard manufacturer, Keen Robinson & Company is bought out. The company had made their mustard a household name and were thought to be at the root of the well-known saying 'keen as mustard'.

1907

John Hertz founds the Yellow Cab Company. Today, there are more than 12,000 taxi cabs registered in New York, making some two hundred million journeys every year. Hertz chose yellow as the colour for his cabs after reading that research carried out by the University of Chicago that yellow was the colour that catches the eye first.

1913

Colman's form an alliance with Reckitts, another industrial conglomerate, to delve into the South American market.

1919

Eugene Christophe becomes the first person to don the Tour de France's famous 'yellow jersey', after winning one of the stages midway through the race. The inaugural Tour de France in 1903 was won by Maurice Garin, who won three of the Tour's six stages. Only in 1919 was the idea of the jersey hit upon, though; yellow to match the colour of the newspaper, *L'Auto* that sponsored the race.

1926

The Mustard Club advertising campaign is launched, aimed at reminding the customer of the exclusive nature of the product.

1938

Reckitt & Colman is created with the amalgamation of both companies. This industrial conglomerate covers many fields including pharmaceuticals, household products and food.

1939

In an amazing, vaudevillian, technicolour whirl, The Wizard of Oz was released, one of Hollywood's most exuberant and imaginative films ever, and Munchkins, wicked witches and the Yellow Brick Road swiftly entered into the lexicon of film.

1952

The first appearance of Sooty on our TV screens, the handpuppet bear operated by Harry Corbett. Corbett bought the puppet from the window of a novelty shop along Blackpool Pier.

1953

The School Crossing Patrol Act is established to allow School Crossing Patrols, or, as they are more affectionately known, lollipop men and women, the power to help children cross the road with safety. The lollipop refers to the high-visibility yellow signs carried by each SCP. Today, there are approximately 30,000 SCPs employed by UK local authorities.

1963

The first hot, ready-mixed mustard is launched.

1966

The first edition of the Yellow Pages is issued, as part of a section of the Brighton telephone directory. 'Yellow Submarine' by The Beatles tops the charts. Later this year, Donovan's 'Mellow Yellow' makes it into the Top 10. The latter is inspired by the Beatles' track and includes Paul McCartney on backing vocals (Donovan had sung backing vocals on 'Yellow Submarine'.)

1970

Football's first yellow card is issued in the game between Mexico and Russia at the Mexico World Cup. During the quarter final of the 1966 World Cup, the diminutive German referee, Kreitlein, had decided to dismiss the huge captain of Argentina. When the Argentinian refused to leave the field, Head of referees, Ken Ashton, left his seat in the stands and made his way onto the pitch to intervene, and the Argentinian duly made for the dressing rooms. Ashton knew the system needed changing, and so thought up the system of yellow (caution) and red (stop!) cards whilst he was passing by a set of traffic lights.

1973

Colman's celebrate 150 years of business, dating back to the first partnership. To commemorate the occasion, they open the Mustard Shop in Norwich, which will go on to become a much-visited, much-loved tourist attraction.

1986

Matt Greoning starts drawing yellow-skinned characters in his notebooks. The following year his cartoons appear as shorts on *The Tracy Ulman Show*. In 1989, on 17th December, the first episode of *The Simpsons* airs on the US Fox Network, and a worldwide phenomenon is born.

1991

The world's most expensive land art project, 'Umbrellas', by the American artist Christo, is staged. It involved the opening of 1,340 huge yellow umbrellas across farmland in California, and an additional 1,760 blue umbrellas in Japan. The project cost $23 million

1995

Colman's is bought by Unilever, one of the world's largest consumer goods firms. Colman's starts to enjoy a new growth cycle.

1996

The Farmyard advertising campaign is developed, featuring animatronic farmyard animals, including a farmyard rendition of 'Staying Alive'.

2000

On April 11th, at London's Millennium Dome, the largest custard-pie fight ever staged commenced, with 3,312 pies thrown by twenty people in the space of three minutes.

2001

Editorial published by the *Observer* newspaper states that there have been over 300 banana-related accidents occurring across the country, this year, most involving people slipping on skins.

2004

Colman's is* 190 years old. Four limited-edition vintage tins are launched to commemorate the fact.

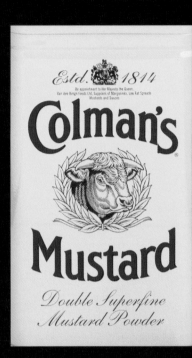

Author's acknowledgments

Where do I start to say thank you to the many friends who have cooked with me, sampled with me and helped to create this book? Firstly, then, to Lynda, my wife, whose unending support means the world to me. A huge thank you to Andy Jones, who is Head Chef at the Slab House in Wells. Andy, just like me, is a real foodie and his input and experiments have really helped to make this book a celebration of one of England's finest food icons. Andy has spent many valuable hours working with me and a jar of mustard, and has produced miracles. Then there is Sarah Francis, a tutor at Whatley Grange Cookery School in Somerset. It is Sarah's sound technical ability that has fine-tuned my cooking and kept me on the straight and narrow. (I can still hear her saying 'Colman's and what?') With reference to technical skills, I must thank Mike Inchbald. Mike is very much part of our company and his huge IT skills made the task of presenting this book ready to the publisher a pleasure rather than a frustration. My friends, who were keen as mustard to help, include Frank Higgins, Peter Nunn, Joanne Myram and our countryman Tony – to all a big thank you. Last, but by no means least, thank you to the publishing team at Absolute Press – Jon Croft (the boss), Meg Avent and Matt Inwood. As with every book they publish, they have done a really superb job in presenting *The Colman's Mustard Cookbook*. May we work together for many years to come?

Publisher's thanks

Thanks to Unilever Bestfoods UK Ltd – especially Clare, Erin, Sarah and Isobel, and to Lesley at the Unilver Archive. Thanks also to Robert Opie and to Caroline at the Kobal Collection.

Permissions and credits

Images on p8, p17, p21, p25, p31, p45, p47, p48, p49, p55, p61, p65, p69, p74 all courtesy of The Ropert Opie Collection. All film images courtesy of The Kobal Collection: p13 MGM / The Kobal Collection; p15 Warner Bros / The Kobal Collection; p23 MGM / The Kobal Collection; p24 Universal / The Kobal Collection; p26 British Lion / The Kobal Collection; p29 MGM / The Kobal Collection; p41 Universal / The Kobal Collection; p52 First National / The Kobal Collection; p63 Paramount / The Kobal Collection; p71 Universal / The Kobal Collection. All other images courtesy and © Unilever Archives and Unilever Bestfoods Ltd.